INTRODUCTION

KU-364-921

The castles, palaces, churches, town halls and monuments of Great Britain are invariably store houses of heraldry. Coats of arms carved in stone, wrought in marble, painted and fashioned in stained glass make them more splendid and tantalise the inquisitive mind. What do they mean? Why are they there? These are questions frequently posed but rarely answered, for heraldry is a specialised study and often the guide books gloss over it, leaving the reader unenlightened.

In this book I am going to examine the royal heraldry of Great Britain, for it is the royal arms, badges and emblems which are most frequently displayed. For centuries people have erected representations of the royal arms to symbolise their loyalty to the Crown or to commemorate a royal connexion or benefaction. It is traditional to mark personal property with heraldic emblems, and, as the property of the Crown has been so widespread and considerable, it is scarcely surprising that the heraldry of the Crown is equally widespread. Royal churches, tombs and monuments bedight with heraldry abound, and, because of their historic and popular interest, tend to be preserved and much visited by the public. Even the thirsty traveller is more likely to end up at an inn called the "King's Arms" than at almost any other and, unless he refreshes himself too liberally, he will doubtless wonder which king the inn sign commemorates.

King Henry VIII decorated Hampton Court Palace with a series of carved beasts symbolising in their heraldry his marriage to Jane Seymour, the mother of King Edward VI. Inspired by this idea and also by the beasts which adorn the roof of St. George's Chapel, Windsor, those who planned the Coronation of Queen Elizabeth II in 1953 commissioned a new set of beasts to illustrate, with heraldic emblems, the Queen's royal ancestry. This happy idea revived interest in royal beasts and badges, and indeed in royal heraldry generally. So in this book I have not only traced the history of the royal arms but also given an account of the three well known groups of royal beasts.

Opposite: The arms of King Henry VI and his queen, Margaret of Anjou. The latter impales the Royal arms of England with her own quartered shield showing Hungary, Naples, Jerusalem, Anjou, Bar and Lorraine.

Front cover: An extract from the 'Armorial Register of the Sovereigns and Knights of the Most Noble Order of the Garter' in the Royal Library, Windsor Castle. It depicts the Royal arms of George IV and, from left to right: Bernard, Duke of Saxe-Meiningen, Prince George of Cumberland, Prince George of Cambridge, Augustus, Duke of Brunswick-Lüneburg, William Duke of Wurtemberg, Duke of Bedford, Duke of Norfolk, Earl Grey, Duke of Grafton, Duke of Buccleuch, Duke of Hamilton, Marquess of Lansdowne, Earl of Carlisle, Duke of Somerset. Reproduced by Gracious Permission of Her Majesty Queen Elizabeth II.
In the margin are Mary I's Tudor rose and sheaf of arrows badge, a banner of the arms of the King of France and a flag with Yorkist falcon and fetterlock badge.

Right: A unicorn argent armed, crined, unguled, gorged and chained or, one of the supporters of the Royal arms adopted since the union of the English and Scottish Crowns. This is in the form of one of the Queen's Beasts (see p. 20) holding a shield bearing the tressured lion of the King of Scots.

HERALDRY

It is not my intention to give a discourse on heraldry. Sufficient to state that distinctive devices painted on shields were first used by nobles and knights some hundred years after the Norman Conquest of 1066. The purpose of these decorative symbols was to identify the bearer in an attractive and dramatic way. For this reason early shields were adorned with bold, simple and symbolic designs. Because these symbols also decorated the coat armour, the loose coat worn over the mail, they came to be called "coats of arms" or just "arms". Obviously the principal value of a coat of arms lay in each coat being peculiar to one person so that positive identification was always possible. Equally, the designs had to be bold and clear in order to be easily seen from afar: this argued a disciplined art-form. In short, someone had to exercise control in order to avoid duplication of arms and the adoption of indifferent designs. Someone had to make rules: make the system work. The people who emerged to undertake these tasks were those most concerned in marshalling the nobility at tournaments and ceremonies, the heralds.

The heralds were officials whose job was to act as messengers and marshals. It was they who were most concerned with identifying the knights and so they had a natural interest in this new fashion of bearing coats of arms. The heralds developed their special knowledge to such an extent that the royal heralds soon emerged as the officers who had control of coats of arms under the Crown. It was because they were so preoccupied with coats of arms that the study of arms came to be called heraldry. Today, as in past ages, the thirteen kings, heralds and pursuivants of arms, generically called heralds, or more correctly, officers of arms, still exercise armorial authority. They are still part of the royal household and they keep their records at the College of Arms in Queen Victoria Street, London. This building stands on a site given to the heralds by King Philip and Queen Mary in 1555 when they were incorporated by Royal Charter, the charter under which they still act.

Left: Garter stall plate of Sir Gilbert Talbot, K.G., Lord Talbot. Above: Officers of Arms including the author (second left) on the steps of the College of Arms.

Symbolism is as old as mankind, so what is it that makes heraldry different from other and more ancient forms of personal and corporate symbolism? Heraldry has developed its own particular characteristics which may briefly be enumerated thus: firstly, it is a form of symbolic display which follows certain conventions and is controlled by responsible officers: secondly, the principal vehicle for the display of the symbols is the shield: thirdly, it is in the nature of an honour, arms being regarded as the insignia or outward sign of gentility. As the Crown is the fount of all honour, arms stem from the Crown and are protected by it. Lastly, arms are hereditary. They are inherited in much the same way as a surname, the only difference being that younger sons add marks of difference to their paternal coat to demonstrate their position in the family.

Obviously before heraldry, as defined above, became firmly rooted as an accepted institution, there was a period of development or pre-heraldry. The knights depicted in the Bayeux Tapestry were accorded decorated shields but these seem to have followed no rules and there is certainly no evidence that they were regarded as being hereditary.

THE ROYAL ARMS – RICHARD I to ELIZABETH I

Geoffrey, Count of Anjou, who was the second husband of Maud, daughter of King Henry I, and thus the ancestor of those Kings of England called Plantagenet, bore golden lions on a blue shield. It is related in a chronicle that when he married in 1127 his father-in-law gave him a shield on which were little lions. When he died in 1151 he was commemorated by a splendid enamel, still to be seen in the museum at Le Mans in Normandy, which shows him bearing a blue shield on which four golden rampant lions

at the birth of heraldry the lion was the favoured beast of the English royal family. It is not therefore surprising that when Richard I had a new Great Seal struck sometime after 1195 it showed him on horseback with a shield on which three lions passant guardant are clearly depicted. The arms of England had been devised and have remained unaltered ever since. The proper heraldic description of the arms is: gules, three lions passant guardant in pale or. That is, on a red shield three golden lions walking along,

Left: the arms of England, 'Gules three lions passant guardant or' as first used by Richard I and by all subsequent sovereigns.

The arms of France (ancient): 'Azure, semy of fleurs-de-lys or'. Charles V of France reduced the number of fleurs-de-lys to three and this was followed by Henry IV.

are visible, a further two probably being hidden by the curve of the shield. There is no evidence that Henry II, Geoffrey's son, used this coat of arms so we cannot say that the coat was hereditary and therefore true heraldry.

Henry's son John (later to be King John) used a seal as Lord of Ireland and Count of Mortain on which two lions are depicted on his shield, and John's elder brother Richard is shown on his first great seal, cut when he came to the throne in 1189, as bearing a lion rampant on his shield. As only one half of his convex shield is visible we do not know whether there was another lion on the other half of the seal.

There is an equestrian seal extant of William FitzEmpress, who died in 1163, younger brother of Henry II, which clearly shows a lion on the shield and on the horse trappings.

William Longespee, Earl of Salisbury, the bastard son of Henry II, bore his grandfather Geoffrey's coat. This is still to be seen, beautifully sculptured, on his tomb in Salisbury Cathedral.

Then there are the two golden lions passant guardant on a red shield which were borne by Henry, Count Palatine of the Rhine, in 1195. Henry was the son of Henry II's daughter Maud. From these evidences it seems clear that

Edward III who claimed the throne of France, quartered the French royal arms with his own.

NT BENEDICT SCHOOL
DERBY

3

The armorial bearings and badges of Henry VI, Edward IV, Richard III and Henry VII from Prince Arthur's Book compiled before 1519. (College of Arms – Vincent MS 152 pp 53-4).

one above the other looking outwards. In the early days of heraldry a lion in this position was called a leopard but this term led to confusion so the expression passant and later passant guardant was used. The brave lion of England was never the cowardly pard!

Kings Henry III, Edward I, Edward II and Edward III until 1340 all used the simple arms of England. In 1340 Edward III quartered with the arms of England those of France, a blue shield strewn with gold fleurs-de-lys. 'Quartered' means that Edward divided his shield into four quarters and placed the arms of France in the first and last quarters (a shield is 'read' from left to right like a book) and those of England in the other two. This method of

depicting two coats on one shield was first noted in England in the arms of Queen Eleanor, first wife of King Edward I and daughter of King Ferdinand III of Castile and Leon. On her arms the castle of Castile was quartered with the lion of Leon.

The reason why Edward quartered the fleurs-de-lys of France was because he claimed the throne of France in the right of his mother Isabella, only daughter and eventually sole heir of King Philip IV of France. Edward's claim was based on the theory that although a woman could not succeed to the throne of France, it could pass through her to her son. The French did not agree and the Hundred Years War began.

In the representation of the royal arms which appears on Edward's third Great Seal the shield is surmounted by a helmet. On the helmet is a chapeau or cap upon which a crowned lion stands. This device, modelled on top of the helm, is called a crest. Curiously, Richard I in his second Great Seal is shown wearing a helm surmounted by a fan on which a lion is depicted. One might be tempted to call this a crest but, in fact, the modelled crest does not really emerge for another hundred years. It became popular during the long reign of Edward III and was soon regarded

Some royal badges: the compound badge of rose and pomegranate of Henry VIII and Catherine of Aragon, the crowned portcullis and sunburst badges of Henry VII, the 'planta genista' badge of Henry II, the star and crescent of Richard I and the 'rose-en-soleil' – the sun of York – badge of Edward IV.

as a secondary hereditary device. When arms were shown two-dimensionally, or on a seal, the helm with crest was frequently shown above the shield, as was the short cloak or 'mantling', which was attached to the helmet and flowed out behind it. This cloak has been a great boon to artists, who by rendering it in a myriad fantastic ways have been able to endow heraldic design with infinite variety.

Edward's son, Edward Prince of Wales, better known as the Black Prince, never lived to inherit the throne but he deserves mention, as his armorial surcoat, the oldest known, is still preserved in Canterbury Cathedral, as is his magnificent crested helm. They provide us with living examples of the vigorous heraldry of an age when it was still used in battle. See page 7.

Although Richard II, the Black Prince's son, used the same arms as his grandfather he also sometimes used a shield augmented with the arms of St. Edward the Confessor. How could this be, for as we have seen no king bore proper heraldic arms until the reign of King Richard I? The answer is that the heralds, steeped in the romantic fancies of the late 13th and early 14th centuries, fancies which drew heavily upon the legends of King Arthur and his Round Table and culminated in the foundation of the Most Noble Order of the Garter, invented arms for pre-heraldic monarchs. These arms are called 'attributed arms'. Of these fanciful coats none is more famous than that of St. Edward the Confessor. This was probably due partly to Edward's standing in the line of kings and partly because the coat assigned to him reflected an actual design which appeared on the reverse of a penny minted in his reign. This consisted of a narrow cross between four birds.

Below: arms of Henry VIII impaling those of Catherine of Aragon.

The arms of Anne Boleyn (above) and (below) Jane Seymour.

The 'arms' of Edward, as they appear impaling the royal arms of Richard II on the reverse of the Wilton Diptych, consist of a cross patonce between five martlets, all in gold on a blue background. This beautiful coat has become so closely connected with Edward's Abbey of Westminster that if forms part of several genuine coats of arms. For example, it occurs in that of the City of Westminster and also in the arms of Ampleforth Abbey, which claims to be the successor of the Abbey of St. Peter at Westminster.

Henry IV, who succeeded Richard, though not the

Right: the seal of Philip and Mary.

5

dynastic heir, bore the same royal coat of France and England quartered. When Henry's second Great Seal was struck in 1405 he altered the arms of France, as King Charles V of France is first said to have done, by reducing the number of fleurs-de-lys to three.

A popular fourteenth century legend told how, in the year 496, a hermit gave Queen Clothilde a holy cloth on which were three lilies, the lily being the symbol of the Blessed Virgin. The queen gave the cloth to King Clovis, her husband. We do not know whether this legend influenced King Charles to abandon the blue shield powdered with lilies but it is at least possible.

After this the Royal Arms of England remained unaltered until the death of Queen Elizabeth, except that King Philip and Queen Mary used a conjugal coat on the Great Seal which was struck after their marriage. The arms on the seal are curious. The shield is divided down the centre by a vertical line: on the right, which is the heraldic left or sinister, as a shield is always described as if one were holding it not looking at it, are Mary's royal arms. On the dexter, the heraldic right side, the dexter half only of Philip's rather complex coat is shown. Presumably this was done simply because, as in Mary's arms, the same

Standard of Henry IV.

coats are repeated twice.

In the first quarter of Philip's arms are the punning coats of Castile and Leon, as borne by Queen Eleanor, quartering the coats of Aragon (the vertical stripes) and Sicily (the stripes and eagles). In the second quarter is the fess (a broad horizontal band) on red for Austria: the arms of France within a border for Burgundy: the bends (diagonal stripes) within a border, the ancient coat of Burgundy and the golden lion on black of Brabant. Over these quarterings is a shield on which is the black lion on gold of Flanders, side by side with the red eagle on silver of Tyrol. In a little point at the base of the shield is the pomegranate which is the symbol of Granada.

The badge and motto of the Prince of Wales is flanked by the Black Prince's shield for peace (left) and the arms of one of his illegitimate sons, Sir Roger de Clarendon. Between the swan badge of Henry V and Richard II's hart is the red hand of Ulster.

THE ROYAL CREST

Although the arms of England remained unaltered for almost two hundred years the crest varied slightly. Edward III, as has been stated, sported a lion, crowned with an open crown standing on a chapeau. Curiously the lion does not look straight ahead over the visor of the helmet but its head is turned to look sideways like the lions on the shield. This must have been artistic licence but it was a fashion which persisted and the royal crest has remained a lion passant guardant ever since.

but from the time of King Henry VIII the lion has invariably stood upon and been crowned with an arched royal crown.

Top: crests of the Coburg family. Above: the crests of the Sovereign as used in England (left) and Scotland. Right: replica of the Black Prince's crest and helm in position above his tomb in Canterbury Cathedral.

It would be illogical actually to wear a crest of a lion looking sideways and the fact that the lion on the Black Prince's helm in Canterbury Cathedral looks forwards, certainly suggests that this is how it was used in tournament and battle.

It will be noted that the Black Prince's original lion has lost its crown, but this has been restored on the replica (right).

Minor variations in the crest occur during the fifteenth century, for example a version of Edward IV's crest shows an uncrowned lion standing within a coronet on a chapeau,

THE ROYAL CROWN

The crown itself has been represented in a variety of ways, as is evidenced by coins, seals and monuments. Generally speaking, until the reign of Henry VI, the royal diadem was an open circlet adorned with fleurs-de-lys or stylised leaves. On Henry VI's first seal for foreign affairs the crown shows crosses formy as part of the decoration of the circlet and these then, with the fleurs-de-lys, became a feature of the royal crown. On Edward IV's third Great Seal an arched crown is shown and in the reign of Henry VII a double arched crown, the arches springing from

Left: St. Edward's Crown.
Right: Charles II's Crown.

crosses formy and fleurs-de-lys, set alternately upon the rim appear on his Great Seal. On the other hand variants of this design feature on coins of the reign.

One depicts a rim set about with ornamental leaves with an arch surmounted by an orb and cross: another shows

Crown Copyright Reserved

Sovereign's crown used at coronations.

two arches springing from pearls and fleurs-de-lys. It was not until the reign of Henry VIII that a jewelled circlet, adorned with four crosses formy and as many fleurs-de-lys was invariably used. Even then the number of arches varied until the end of the 17th century. Sometimes two arches were shown and sometimes only one, springing from the crosses, but the arches were invariably

surmounted at their intersection by an orb ensigned with a cross formy.

The heraldic royal crown which has been used since the end of the 17th century is based on that made by Sir Robert Vyner for the coronation of King Charles II in 1662. It is sometimes called St. Edward's Crown and is the symbol of sovereignty. It is all of gold, the rim being studded with pearls and showing a sapphire between two emeralds and at either end a ruby.

There are two arches, one and a half being visible. It is now usual to show on the outer arch nine large pearls on either side of the central orb whilst on the centre arch,

Prince of Wales' coronet.

Below: Henry IV's crown on his effigy in Canterbury Cathedral.

Coronet used by Sovereign's daughters and younger sons.

Coronet used by children of the heir-apparent.

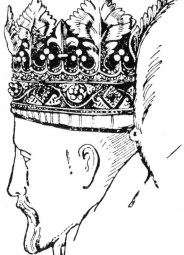

Coronet used by children of sons (other than the heir-apparent) and brothers of the Sovereign.

being in perspective, only five pearls are shown. The orb, symbolising the world, is usually coloured green, the bands, and cross above it being gold. A cap of crimson velvet turned up with ermine, is frequently shown within the crown.

Although the above specifications have pertained during this century the shape of the crown has varied. In that favoured by the present queen the arches are depressed in the centre but Kings Edward VII, George V and George VI all used a crown with the arches bent like bows. An early crown associated with Queen Victoria dispenses with the pearls on the arches, replacing them with ornamental gold foliage.

Although the heralds may have shaken their heads sadly at the use of such an 'improper' crown, they could not say it was wrong of the queen to use it, for in matters heraldic the sovereign is the ultimate law.

THE ROYAL SUPPORTERS

During the second half of the 15th century artists and seal engravers began to augment coats of arms by placing two creatures on either side of the shield. At first these seem to have been chosen capriciously and were not regarded as an integral part of the coat of arms. However, as they increased in popularity and as they literally supported the shield, the heralds began to take notice of them and eventually formulated rules for their control and inheritance.

It is both difficult and dangerous to make sweeping generalisations about the use of supporters but it is fair to say that during the 15th century they were sometimes used but not taken too seriously. They consisted of favourite beasts and badges put to a new and attractive use. It was left to the Tudor heralds, emancipated from the blood bath of civil strife, peacefully to rationalise their use and bring them within the confines of strict armorial practice.

It must here be appreciated that quite apart from formal armorial bearings, that is shield of arms, crest, and later supporters, the greater nobility freely used armorial devices as motifs in decoration and as badges with which they marked their property and retainers. Such use was often free and fantastical, but it was as much part of the mediaeval scene as the masque, miracle play, fair or tournament. It is therefore difficult to draw the line between an artistic embellishment and a truly armorial supporter.

An heraldic antelope and a swan have been attributed to Henry IV and an antelope and a lion to him and his son Henry V. Antelopes, lions and panthers have all been associated with Henry VI. To Edward IV are accorded two white lions, a lion and hart and a lion and a black bull. Richard III has two white boars, and a lion and a boar. It is not until the reign of Henry VII that there is good contemporary evidence for the more or less consistent use of supporters by the sovereign, although the actual beasts vary. Henry VII's grandfather, Owen Tudor, used a red dragon garnished with gold as a badge, claiming descent from Cadwalader, the last native ruler of Britain, to whom a dragon was attributed. It is not surprising, therefore, to find that Henry greatly favoured this beast. He used it as a badge and also as a supporter to his arms: he even created a new pursuivant (the junior rank of herald) whom he named Rouge Dragon. Henry used the dragon as his dexter supporter in conjunction with a greyhound. He also used two greyhounds, witness the representation of his arms at the Bishop's Palace, Exeter.

The greyhound was a popular badge of the Lancastrian kings and when Henry VI created his half-brother Edmund Tudor, Earl of Richmond, he also assigned him his white greyhound badge as a supporter. It is not surprising that Henry should have attached especial importance to this royal beast, which he would have inherited from his father, for it symbolised, and perhaps in his eyes made more substantial, his tenuous links with the house of Lancaster.

King Henry VIII, like his father, did not just use two supporters. He rang the changes but generally favoured the crowned golden lion as his dexter and the red dragon as his sinister supporter, which is probably why King

Edward VI, Queen Mary I and Queen Elizabeth I, who made the dragon gold, all used these supporters: except that Mary, when bearing her arms conjoined to those of

Arms used on Her Majesty's Great Seal for Scotland.

King Philip gave her husband his black eagle in place of her dragon.

In 1603 James VI of Scotland came to the throne as James I of England. As king of Scots his arms were supported by two silver unicorns with golden horns, manes, beards, tufts and hooves. About the neck of each was a golden circlet like that in the royal crown and attached to this was a gold chain reflexed over the monster's back. King James kept the English lion supporter but banished the red dragon in favour of one of his Scottish unicorns. The lion and the unicorn have been the royal supporters ever since.

Henry VII's dragon and greyhound.

Arms of the Stuart Kings after 1603, WIlliam III and Queen Anne after 1707.

THE ROYAL ARMS OF THE STUARTS

When James became king he not only introduced the unicorn but altered the royal arms to demonstrate that he was also King of Scots.

King Henry VIII was styled King of Ireland from 1542, having previously, as the former kings, been styled 'Lord of Ireland': but he bore no arms to represent his new kingdom. James put this right by establishing arms for the kingdom, based on the harp badge formerly used to symbolise Ireland.

The arms consisted of a golden harp with silver strings (today seven are usually shown) on a blue background. The shield in James's new version of the royal arms was divided into four quarters; in the first and fourth quarters the old Tudor royal arms were placed, that is France and England quartered; the arms of Scotland were put in the second and those of Ireland in the third quarter. The arms

of Scotland consist of a red lion rampant on a golden shield within a red *double tressure flory counterflory*. This consists of a border round the shield composed of two narrow parallel lines interlaced with fleurs-de-lys pointing alternately inwards and outwards. This coat first appears in about 1235 on the seal of King Alexander II, although the double tressure is not clearly shown as it is in the seal of his son and successor, Alexander III.

The Stuart royal arms continued in use for over a hundred years, until the Act of Union with Scotland in 1707. They were, however, augmented when William III came to the throne in 1689.

William, Prince of Orange, was the son of William II of Orange and Mary, daughter of Charles I. He married Mary, daughter of James II. When James II fled the country and was declared by the Convention Parliament, which met on 22 January, 1689, to have abdicated the government, thereby leaving the throne vacant, William and Mary were declared joint sovereigns.

William had been made Stadtholder, sometimes translated as "chief magistrate", of the United Netherlands and to represent this important position he placed a small shield over the royal arms which he and Mary bore, consisting simply of the arms of Nassau; a blue shield spattered with vertical gold rectangles and a gold lion over all. These arms are still the royal arms of Holland.

After William's death, his sister in law, Queen Anne, removed the arms of Nassau and bore the old Stuart royal arms. In 1707 the kingdoms of England and Scotland were united by "The Act for the Union with Scotland". The kingdom known as Great Britain had been born and to symbolise this, the royal arms were altered.

The arms of England were placed side by side with those of Scotland (like the arms of a married couple) in the first and fourth quarters. France was given the whole of the second and Ireland the entire third quarter.

This version of the royal arms was used until Anne's death in 1714. Although Anne had innumerable children by her husband, Prince George of Denmark, none survived and she was succeeded, under the terms of the Act of Settlement of 1701, by the next Protestant heir, George, Elector of Hanover.

Left: Arms used by Mary Queen of Scots as widow of Francis II, King of France.

10

Sir David Lyndsay of the Mount's version of the arms of King James V of Scots.

1

2

5

KEY

1. Arms attributed to some of the early Norman kings.

2. The 'leopards' of England as first used by Richard I.

3. France (ancient) quartering England adopted by Edward III.

4. France (modern) quartering England as first used by Henry IV.

5. England and France quartering the lion of Scotland and the harp of Ireland. Used by James I.

EVOL
OF
ROYA

7

8

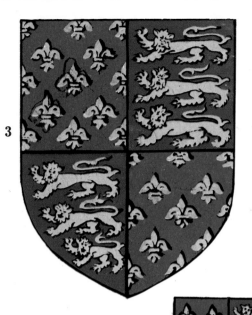

3

4

6

KEY

6. Arms of William III: the Stuart royal arms with Nassau on an inescutcheon.

7. The arms of Queen Anne after 1707.

8. Arms of the Georges until 1801.

9. George III used these arms from 1801 except that the crown was at first an elector's cap until 1816, Hanover having became a kingdom.

10. Arms used by Queen Victoria and all subsequent Sovereigns.

9

10

SAINT BENEDICT SCHOOL
DERBY

13

THE HANOVERIANS AND AFTER

George, a great-grandson of James I, was not only Elector of Hanover, that is one of those princes who elected the Holy Roman Emperor, but also Duke of Brunswick and Lüneburg. So, to symbolise his German dominions and dignities, he substituted German arms for the English and Scottish arms in the fourth quarter of the post-1707 royal arms.

Arms as used by George I quartering Electoral coat and used until 1801.

The new coat was divided into three. In the first third were the two golden lions passant guardant on red of Brunswick. In the second third was shown a blue lion on a golden background spattered with red hearts: the arms of Lüneburg. In the lower third the white horse of Hanover galloped in a red field. In the centre, on a small red shield was a representation of the Crown of Charlemagne, the badge of the Arch-Treasurer of the Holy Roman Empire, an office held by George.

These arms were used by the first three Georges until 1801 when, because of the Act for Union with Ireland, the royal arms were altered yet again. On this occasion the royal arms of France, symbol of an ancient and hollow pretension, were finally removed. The arms of England were placed in the first and fourth quarters, those of Scotland in the second quarter and the harp of Ireland in the third. The German arms were placed on a shield in the centre of the royal arms. This shield was ensigned by the Electoral Bonnet, a crimson cap turned up with ermine, symbol of the electoral dignity.

After the ultimate defeat of Napoleon at Waterloo, the Congress of Vienna, in 1815, resettled the frontiers of Europe. The old Electorate of Hanover was made into a Kingdom, the Holy Roman Empire being no more. George III became the first King of Hanover and in 1816 an arched crown was substituted for the electoral bonnet in the royal arms.

Kings George IV and William IV, both kings of Hanover, used the same arms. But, when William IV died in 1837 and was succeeded by his niece Victoria, the crowns were divided. A woman could not rule in Hanover, so that the crown passed to William's next living brother, Ernest Duke of Cumberland and Queen Victoria removed the German arms from the royal arms. The result was the royal arms as we know them today.

Opposite: Arms of George IV. The Orders represented below the motto are those of St Patrick, Bath, Garter, Thistle and Guelph.

Below left: Arms used after 1801 showing electoral cap altered to a crown in 1816, Hanover having become a kingdom.

Below: Arms as used with slight variations from the accession of Queen Victoria to the present day.

ROYAL HELMS, MANTLINGS, MOTTOES AND INSIGNIA

In the foregoing account of the royal arms I have not mentioned what may be called the 'trimmings', namely the royal helm, mantling and motto and insignia of the Order of the Garter.

DIEV ET MON DROIT

The royal helm was an ordinary steel helm, sometimes embellished with gold, until Queen Elizabeth I introduced the gold barred helm facing the front which was used thereafter.

Elizabeth's taste for gold also found expression in the mantling. Previous monarchs had used a red mantling lined with ermine but Elizabeth substituted gold for red and so it has remained.

The well known royal motto *Dieu et mon droit* (my God and my right) has been used since the time of King Henry V. His father Henry IV and his brother the Duke of Bedford used the word *Souverayne* (Sovereign) and some other monarchs have used different mottoes. Queens Elizabeth I and Anne favoured *Semper eadem* (Always the same). Mary I used *Veritas temporis filia* (Truth is the daughter of Time). James I sometimes used *Beati pacifici* (Blessed are the peacemakers) and William III's motto was *Je maintiendrai* (I shall maintain).

Shields of arms are often seen encircled by a blue Garter, ornamented with gold and inscribed with the legend *Honi soit qui mal y pense* (Evil be to him who evil thinks). This means that the bearer of the arms is a knight of the Most

Noble Order of the Garter, founded by King Edward III in about 1348. The Garter is part of the insignia with

Right: helm, mantling, crest and ostrich-feather badge of Richard II.

Left: arms of James I from Gwillim's 'Display of Heraldry' 1610.

Below: insignia of the Most Noble Order of the Garter.

which a knight is invested and, since the reign of Henry VIII, the Sovereign and Knights Companion of the Order have encircled their arms with a representation of it.

THE KING'S BEASTS

Reference has been made to royal beasts and badges. If these were to be listed and described in detail a weighty tome would be needed to do them justice, but there are certain well-known series of beasts, badges and arms which, if described, will go some way to enlightening the reader on this fascinating by-way of heraldry.

We know from the building accounts for Hampton Court Palace that, when Henry VIII started to improve, augment and embellish the palace, heraldry played a large part in his schemes. Royal beasts and beasts for Henry's then queen, Anne Bullen or Boleyn, abounded. There were sixteen on the coping stones of the gables of the great hall, sixteen more on the battlements and yet more beasts capped the columns of the louvre and were to be found both within the palace and all over the grounds. Lions, dragons and greyhounds, the supporters of the arms of the first two Tudor monarchs, predominated, whilst Anne's leopard, the dexter supporter of her arms, was also featured. With a few exceptions these beasts held vanes but there is no record as to how these were decorated.

The gardens were being completed in 1536, the year when Anne was executed, her place as queen being taken by Jane Seymour. Unembarrassed, Henry ordered Anne's arms and badges to be replaced by those of Queen Jane and, in the cause of economy, Anne's leopards in the new garden were altered into Jane's panthers by "new makying of hedds and taylls".

To commemorate Henry's marriage to Jane, twelve beasts were set on the parapet of the bridge over the moat. There were two lions, two dragons, two greyhounds, two unicorns, two panthers, a bull and a yale. In the reign of William III the parapet was demolished and the moat filled in, so it is not known what devices these creatures supported. However, excavations in the moat revealed fragments which showed that these beasts held shields not vanes.

In 1909, when the moat was cleared and the bridge restored, it was decided to replace the beasts. As there was only room for ten on the new bridge a king's greyhound and a queen's unicorn were excised by Mr E. E. Dorling who designed them. King and queen were each accorded five beasts and these were disposed alternately on the two parapets. Unfortunately the new beasts did not take kindly to the English climate and in 1950 they were so eroded that

The Yale of Beaufort.   *The Bull of Clarence.*   *Jane Seymour's Unicorn.*

they had to be replaced by the noble creatures now to be seen at Hampton Court.

As one approaches the palace on the left-hand parapet of the bridge the following beasts are to be found:

1. The crowned lion of England, as used by Henry for his dexter supporter, holds a shield of the royal arms impaling (placed side by side with) the six quarterings of Queen Jane (see below).

2. Jane's panther supports a shield of the arms of Seymour, a pair of gold wings, presumably those of a sea-mew, on red. The heraldic panther resembles a leopard which is why it was relatively simple to alter Anne Bullen's leopards to Jane's panthers, but it is covered with spots of divers colours and flames issue from its ears and mouth. Jane's panther, which is collared with a coronet and chained, was the dexter supporter of her arms. It was probably given her by Henry from the treasury of royal beasts, for a panther had been counted among their number since the time of Henry IV and possibly even earlier.

3. The greyhound, a favourite Tudor beast and a supporter of the arms of Henry VII and sometimes of Henry VIII, holds a shield of the arms of England. The greyhound, friend and companion of man, most elegant of canines and symbol of loyalty and celerity, was a beast adopted by Edward III and thereafter used by many of his descendants, particularly those of the House of Lancaster, from which line Henry VII was descended. Henry IV is known to have worn a collar of linked greyhounds and a greyhound is to be found on the Great Seals of Henry V and VI. Edmund Tudor, Earl of Richmond and father of Henry VII was granted a white greyhound as a supporter by his half-brother Henry VI, which is why this beast is

popularly known as the greyhound of Richmond. The beast at Hampton Court is collared and leashed: collared it usually was but leashed never. The inclusion of the leash resulted from a misunderstanding as to the beast's origin.

4. A yale holds a shield of the arms of augmentation granted to Jane by her husband. Henry gave a special 'extra' coat of arms, called an augmentation, to each of his wives other than those of royal birth, Catherine of Aragon and Anne of Cleves. Jane's coat is of gold with a pile, on which are the arms of England, between six blue fleurs-de-lys. The yale is an heraldic antelope which can swivel its horns round to counter attack from all quarters. It has large tusks and is silver bedight with bezants – big gold spots.

Henry IV's son John, Duke of Bedford, was the first to use a yale. We can only hazard a guess as to why he chose this particular beast from the myriad creatures to be found in old bestiaries. One suggestion is that Pliny calls the yale an eale and, as John was also Earl of Kendal – Kend-eale-he used it to pun on the name of his earldom. This is pretty far-fetched but, whatever John's reason for choosing the yale, after his death without issue his cousin Sir John Beaufort, Henry VII's grandfather, was created Earl of Kendal and took the yale as a supporter. From that time it has been regarded as a Beaufort beast.

5. The Tudor dragon, which has been noted before as a favourite supporter, symbolising the supposed ancient, royal, Welsh ancestry of the Tudors, supports a shield on which is an uncrowned portcullis. The portcullis was a Beaufort badge which was adopted by Henry VII and, ensigned by a crown, became one of his favourite badges. It forms a principal motif in the decoration of Henry VII's Chapel in Westminster Abbey and is the royal badge used

| *The Tudor Greyhound* | *Jane Seymour's Panther* | *The Dragon of Wales* |

Hampton Court showing the King's Beasts in situ.

in connexion with the Palace of Westminster. It is also the badge of Somerset Herald (the Beauforts were Dukes of Somerset) and, uncrowned, of Portcullis Pursuivant, a title created by Henry VII.

On the right-hand parapet are the following creatures:

1. A unicorn holding a shield of the full arms of Queen Jane: that is with all her six quarterings. The unicorn is generally regarded as a Scottish royal beast, and so it is, but there is evidence that it was also used by the English royal family. It is mentioned in one or two manuscripts as being a royal badge, which is perhaps why it was given to Jane as her sinister supporter. Also the unicorn is a symbol of purity and fertility. Jane was no courtesan like her predecessor and Henry urgently needed to invoke the gods of fertility to acquire a son: it is tempting to think that it was for this reason he conjured up a relatively little used royal beast.

Jane's arms consist of the arms of augmentation followed by the Seymour arms, both described above. The third quartering, the blue and white fur known as *vair*, is for Beauchamp of Hache: the fourth quartering, three demi-lions rampant on silver is for Sturmy, the fifth of three roses, red on silver and vice versa is for MacWilliams and the last quartering, three gold leopards' faces on a red bend on silver, is for Coker. Jane was descended from heiresses of all these families.

2. Another royal dragon supports Henry's royal arms of France and England quartered.

3. A lion of England, only crowned with a coronet rather than an arched crown, holds a shield on which is Jane's elaborate badge. The badge almost defies description, illustration being more eloquent than words. The crowned hawthorn bush refers to the Tudor badge, which is composed of such a bush either with or without a crown in its midst. The allusion is to Richard's III's crown being found by Lord Stanley in a hawthorn bush after the battle of Bosworth. The noble lord saw fit to remove it and place it on the head of Henry Tudor.

4. The black bull of Clarence bears a shield on which is the badge of a Tudor rose. When the houses of York and Lancaster were united by the marriage of Henry VII and Elizabeth of York, daughter of Edward IV, this was symbolised by joining the red rose of Lancaster to the white rose of York. This was effected in various ways, but that most favoured by the Tudor monarchs was a white rose in the centre of a red rose, usually ensigned by the royal crown.

The black bull was used as a badge by Lionel Duke of Clarence, second son of Edward III, ancestor of the Yorkist kings. In this way it became a royal badge. It may originally have been used as a badge by the Clares, whose honour (a complex of many manors) of Clare or Clarence came to Lionel through his wife Elizabeth de Burgh.

5. The queen's panther this time holds a shield of her conjugal arms, shown in the same way as on the first shield, supported by the royal lion.

THE QUEEN'S BEASTS

An equally interesting series of royal beasts is that devised for Her Majesty the Queen on the occasion of her coronation in 1953. The idea of producing a new series of beasts was that of the then Garter King of Arms, Sir George Bellew. He asked me to ferret around and make some suggestions. This I did and came up with a tentative scheme, the basic idea being to illustrate the Queen's ancestry with beasts and badges. My first thoughts were then reconsidered by Mr. Hugh Stanford London, later Norfolk Herald Extraordinary, and a definite plan was put before Sir George Bellew for his approval. When the beasts had been approved they were sculptured by Mr. James Woodford, O.B.E., R.A., and were placed outside the entrance to Westminster Abbey. Later small models appeared, rendered in a variety of materials, and a fine new set was carved in Portland stone and can now be seen in Kew Gardens. These beasts have become part of history and reproductions of them are still popular. Many of the Queen's Beasts and the emblems they hold have been described above but others will need detailing. I shall consider the beasts in their genealogical order and, because I was intimately concerned with their genesis, must ask to be forgiven if this account is written from a somewhat personal point of view.

1. The earliest royal beast was the lion, so the lion of England, now crowned as is the royal supporter, holds the royal arms of the Queen: thus the continuity of the monarchy is symbolised by the noble lion, England's and also Scotland's pre-eminent royal beast.

2. We sought a beast, other than the lion, to represent Edward III who sired the dynasties of York and Lancaster and we found a griffin. Of all the creatures attributed to Edward, the griffin seemed the most personal, for on Edward's signet, or private seal, was a griffin. The griffin, which has the head, only with ears, foreparts and wings of an eagle and the hindparts of a lion, holds a shield on which is the newest royal badge, that of the House of Windsor.

In 1917 King George V proclaimed that his Royal House and family should be named Windsor and his son, George VI, instituted a badge for the newly named royal House in 1938. It consists of the round tower of Windsor Castle on a mount and with the royal banner flying above it, all between two branches of oak ensigned by the royal crown.

3. The next three beasts have Yorkist connexions, for although the Lancastrians seized the throne, the senior heir was Roger Mortimer, Earl of March, the son of Lionel Duke of Clarence's heiress Philippa, and whose daughter

The Yale of Beaufort with crowned portcullis badge.

The Lion of England bearing the Royal arms of the United Kingdom.

The Black Bull of Clarence bearing the Royal arms as used from 1405 to 1603.

Centre: the Griffin of Edward III displaying the badge of the Royal House of Windsor.

Below: the White Lion of Mortimer bearing a Yorkist badge – the white rose 'en soleil'.

Above: the Falcon of the Plantagenets bearing the golden fetterlock badge.

and co-heir Anne married her cousin Richard, the Duke of York's brother, the ancestor of the Yorkist kings.

Although the silver falcon was used by Edward III, it became a Yorkist creature and was used often within a golden fetterlock, as in the badge supported by the falcon. The shield on which this badge is displayed is parted of the Yorkist colours, blue and murrey – the colour of the juice of mulberry berries.

4. The history of the black bull of Clarence has been told. Here he holds the royal arms as used between about 1405 and 1603.

5. The Yorkist claim to the throne came through the family of Mortimer and so the white lion of Mortimer, an ancient badge of that family, occurs holding a shield, parted of the Yorkist colours, like that held by the falcon, but emblazoned with another Yorkist badge, the white rose *en soleil*, that is shown against a sun. The sun was a badge of Richard II, who named Roger Mortimer heir to the throne.

SAINT BENEDICT SCHOOL DERBY

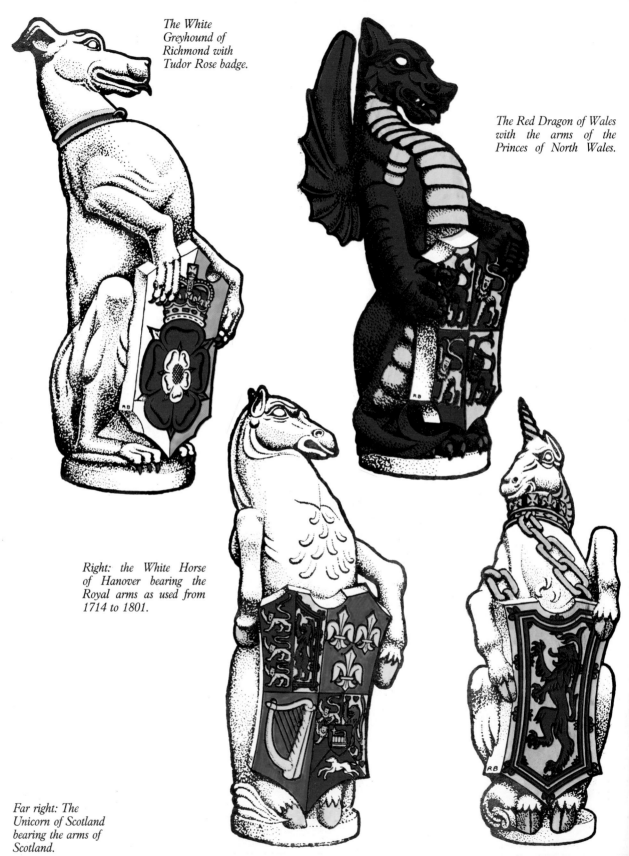

The White Greyhound of Richmond with Tudor Rose badge.

The Red Dragon of Wales with the arms of the Princes of North Wales.

Right: the White Horse of Hanover bearing the Royal arms as used from 1714 to 1801.

Far right: The Unicorn of Scotland bearing the arms of Scotland.

6. Having commemorated the House of York, the House of Lancaster is represented by the Yale of Beaufort supporting a shield of the Beaufort livery colours, blue and white, emblazoned with the crowned portcullis badge. Both beast and badge have been previously noted.

7. The greyhound of Richmond, here correctly depicted without a leash, holds a shield of the Tudor rose badge. It is shown ensigned with the royal crown on a shield parted of the Tudor livery colours of silver and green.

8. York and Lancaster were united in the Tudors, but this family had a personality of its own, a personality which was essentially Welsh. The next beast is therefore the red dragon, about which much has already been written, here holding the arms of the old princes of North Wales, of whom Llewelyn the Great was recognised as ruler of all Wales. The arms consist of a quartered shield of gold and red on which are four lions passant guardant counter-coloured red and gold. In 1911 these arms were assigned to the Prince of Wales to bear, ensigned by his coronet, over the royal arms in order to symbolise the Principality. Prince Charles also bears his arms in this way.

9. The next dynasty, the Stuarts, is best represented by the Scottish unicorn supporter which, appropriately, holds a shield of the old royal arms of Scotland, now the second quartering in the royal arms of the United Kingdom.

10. Finally the House of Hanover is symbolised by the white horse of Hanover holding a shield of the royal arms as borne from the accession of George I in 1714 until the Union with Ireland in 1801. The white horse was originally a Brunswick emblem which became closely associated with Hanover.

THE WINDSOR BEASTS

The last series of beasts worthy of note adorn the roof of St. George's Chapel, Windsor. In the upper tier are forty-two beasts holding vanes and standing on the pinnacles of the clerestory parapet. About twenty-four feet below these stand the remaining beasts supporting shields: twenty-four on the flying buttresses, eight in the niches of the transepts' walls and two on the parapet at the west end. Although there are seventy-six beasts, only fourteen different creatures are represented. Many of these we have seen before: namely, the crowned lion of England supporting the arms of England, the Welsh dragon supporting two Tudor badges conjoined, a portcullis

St. George's Chapel, Windsor Castle, shrine of the Order of the Garter and decorated with the Windsor Beasts.

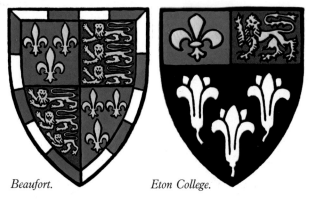

Beaufort.   *Eton College.*   *Nevill.*   *de Bohun.*

placed over a Tudor rose: the Yorkist falcon with the arms of England and the bull of Clarence with the white rose *en soleil.*

Then there are some old friends with new burdens. The panther, here depicted more like the zoological creature, supports the arms granted by King Henry VI to his foundation, Eton College in 1449. On a black shield are three white lilies: the top third of the shield is parted blue and red: on the blue is a gold fleur-de-lys and on the red a lion of England: the Beaufort yale supports the arms of that family, namely the royal arms of France and England quartered all within a border of silver and blue pieces. The Beauforts were the legitimated issue of John of Gaunt, Duke of Lancaster, by Catherine Swynford: the lion of Mortimer holds a shield of the arms of that family. This coat is better illustrated than described. It is all gold and blue, except the little shield which is silver. The Richmond greyhound holds a shield emblazoned with the arms of Nevill, a silver saltire, on red, for the Nevills were much intermarried with the Plantagenets.

There are also six new beasts. There is the famous white swan of Bohun, which has a history going back to the legendary Swan Knight. Henry IV used it in the right of his wife Mary, daughter and one of the heiresses of Humphrey de Bohun, Earl of Hereford, Essex and Northampton. Here it appropriately holds the arms of Bohun: a blue shield, on which is a silver bend between two narrow gold bends and six golden lions.

Richard II's favourite badge was the white hart. It may have been derived from his mother's badge of a hind and was perhaps also intended as a pun on his name Rich-hart. Here it holds a shield on which is the punning Plantagenet badge of broom-pods, the *planta genesta.*

Another Bohun beast was a silver antelope, collared with a golden circlet and chained. It bears the arms of France and England quartered before the number of French lilies was reduced to three. Both antelope and swan became royal beasts after their adoption by Henry IV.

The black dragon was a badge of the Earls of Ulster. This earldom was held by de Burghs from whom descended the Yorkist kings. It is right that it should here support the red cross on gold of de Burgh.

Finally there are two other beasts which carry vanes rather than shields. They are the unicorn of Edward III and the hind of Edward V. It has been mentioned that the unicorn was an English royal beast before James I brought it from Scotland. Quite why it was attributed to Edward III is not known but in an old manuscript a unicorn is

shown next to Edward III's lion: it could be that the attribution is based on this rather flimsy evidence.

Mention has been made of the hind being a badge of Richard II's mother, Joan Holland. Although Richard had no issue, the hind was adopted as a Yorkist badge and it is shown as a supporter of the arms of Edward V in the south aisle of St. George's Chapel.

* * * * * *

As I have mentioned, there are many other royal beasts and badges although the most noted have been described in this book. They can be seen adorning old castles, palaces and public buildings. Collecting details of such beasts and badges makes an interesting and worthwhile hobby, and I hope that this book may prove not just a useful guide but also a reference book for anyone who makes a hobby of the study of royal heraldry and insignia.

Designed and published by Pilgrim Press Ltd., Lodge Lane, Derby.

Printed in Great Britain.

Photographs of the King's Beasts and Hampton Court are Crown copyright and reproduced with permission of Her Majesty's Stationery Office. The standard on page 6 and the arms of Mary Queen of Scots on page 10 are by the late Wilfred Scott-Giles, O.B.E., Fitzalan Pursuivant Extraordinary. The post 1801 arms on page 14 and the Garter insignia on page 16 are from Boutell's 'Heraldry' and reproduced by permission of Messrs. Frederick Warne Ltd. and Penguin Books. The Queen's Beasts are taken from the originals by Robert Brown. The illustration in colour on page 14 is reproduced by permission of the Royal Warrant Holders Association. The illustration on page 1 was drawn by Tom Wrigley.

ISBN 0 900594 59 4

© Pilgrim Press Ltd., 1987.

Opposite: the Windsor Beasts on the parapet of St. George's Chapel, Windsor. By permission of the Dean and Canons.

Back cover: An unusual display of the arms of Elizabeth I showing shields of England, Ireland and Wales and her motto 'Semper Eadem'.